When Family Does You Wrong

Stories of Betrayal, Broken Bonds, Unresolved Differences, Redemption, Forgiveness and Healing

Lorraine Spencer

WHEN FAMILY DOES YOU WRONG

Lorraine Spencer

When Family Does You Wrong

ISBN-13: 978-0615872698

ISBN-10: 0615872697

Acknowledgments

I would like to thank all my extra eyes and reviewers: Tricia Joseph, Robyn Murray, Stella Parker, and Barbara Hakala. I would also like to thank all the contributors for allowing me to share their stories as told to me or submitted to me. I am hoping, as it was in my case, cathartic and a path to healing.

Selena T. Gainor*, you have helped many young women to see that life is much too short to live it trying to please others. You will make a wonderful wife to some lucky fella.

Dr. Misee Harris, faith in God does not equal faith in man. God's message doesn't change because people choose to pervert it or become devils in disguise. I trust that you will find a balance and worship again. You are already a star, so keep looking ahead.

Clarissa Burton, you have been such an inspiration and help to me. You are a terrific storyteller and have an ability to transform your readers into your mind. Your experiences made you the great person you are today.

Terrina Williams*, you are such a strong woman. I am so sorry for your loss and trust that you will eventually be able to heal. You have done so many wonderful things in your life and have a beautiful family. I wish that you can reconnect and be made as whole as much as possible. Keep being a terrific wife and mom!

Trudy Struthers*, thankfully your baby was young enough that he won't remember the episode and the scars most likely went away. You had to protect your children from someone who refused to see her how dangerous her daughter was at the time; but I am glad you have forgiven her. Keep on loving your sister from a distance.

Dennis Stuart*, you are an example of a wonderful husband and father. Your wife is fortunate and blessed. I suspect that some enabling went on but you matured and outgrew the pettiness. You are a testament to how happy one can be once they define purpose and determination in his or her life. Maybe someday your brother will see.

*All names and some details associated in these stories have been changed to protect the privacy of those individuals and their families.

Introduction

In life, we encounter good and bad people. Good people can do bad things some times. Within our lifetimes, we are faced with betrayals, hatred, crime, terrorism and all kinds of evil committed by strangers and so-called friends. But the dagger sticks in a little deeper when a member of one's own family.

Welcome to a series of stories of wrongdoing by family members. Although some of the stories are most certainly heartbreaking, there is sometimes a light at the end of the tunnel. As well, some stories remain unresolved with no closure. You may see yourself in a story, or be familiar with someone in a similar circumstance. Then again you may be shocked or horrified and disgusted, never having imagined that human beings -- family can be so hurtful and in some cases down right evil to one another.

Contents

Foreword

We've often said as well as heard others say, "Blood is thicker than water", referring to our blood relatives or those adopted into our families. This old adage sounds so good rolling off our tongues until reality bites us. Family can bring us the greatest joy. Family can also bring the great pain not even a stranger can outdo. The painful and disappointing family episodes can bring many of us to our knees wondering how those who claim to love and chanted, "Blood is thicker than water" treat us with such disdain without remorse.

Lorraine Spencer has gathered several painful stories from individuals wronged by family members. These stories are heart wrenching and may surprise many readers that such behaviors are possible, especially when perpetrated by the very people we have entrusted our lives to. Most of all, these stories show the courage to tell their sad stories as a warning to others by letting others know they can let go and move on.

Sometimes we must leave family members where they stand. If we don't, our life's purpose may never be fulfilled. Emotional and psychological enslavement by some family members must stop. Of course, blood is thicker than water. But if you continue to bleed, eventually you will die. The stories in this book will encourage you to stand up and speak out. You are worthy.

Clarissa Burton

Devastating Consequences

Just call me "Undeserving". My family is among many who found themselves victims of a devious mortgage scheme. Our story is a little different in that my brother and sister-in-law were the ones who took full advantage of us. The result has been devastation, homelessness, rush to judgment, a rift within our family, and financial ruin. It is bad enough when a stranger takes advantage of, steals from, deceives, and does other horrible things to innocent victims. But when it is a member of your own family, it can be particularly devastating.

In April of 2010, my husband and I were presented with a proposal from my brother Ronnie and sister-in-law Melissa. My little family was living in a cramped two bedroom condo and had long outgrown it by the time our second child was born. My brother and his wife were going to relocate from Loudon County, Virginia to El Paso, Texas with the Department of Defense (DOD). Ronnie asked us if we could afford $2,000 a month for rent until we could purchase their 5 bedroom, two car garage home. My husband and I discussed how we could sacrifice, and decided to jump on the opportunity to move. I was a stay at home mother with significant health challenges on disability, yet I was willing to try and work a part time job, to make moving into our own home easier. My husband and I went to a mortgage company, applied for, and qualified for a loan that was little more than what the home was then valued. We received a preapproval letter, took it to my brother and presented it to him so we would not have to wait to move into the home. We qualified for our dream home and could not have been happier. My children, a son and a daughter, needed their own rooms, and they would have more space than they would know what to do with in their very own home! My husband and I were totally unaware that Ronnie was working with someone whom he thought was a "lawyer."

A man named Chandler Braun promised Ronnie and Melissa that he could get them a loan modification at a percentage rate of two point something or another. According to Ronnie, this Chandler Braun fellow told him that he should "absolutely NOT" sell to us because our realtor only wanted a commission. He advised Ronnie that he should wait until their loan process was complete before selling the house. When Ronnie approached us with the proposal of renting the house instead of buying it, we should have taken our preapproval letter elsewhere right then and there. Had we done so, we might be sitting in our own home today. But I had no reason to think Ronnie or Melissa had an agenda. In June, we decided to go ahead and rent the home for what we thought would be six months and then purchase. So we moved in and paid Ronnie $2,000.00 for the various pieces of broken furniture and appliances Melissa and he had left behind. They cleaned the carpet, but other than that, the place was filthy and the house was in need of repair. The rent of $2,000.00 a month was going to be a struggle, but we were prepared to deal with that because we were going to be in our dream home; or so we thought.

We needed a lease to show proof of residency so our children could register for their new schools. Braun sent one of his partners to the house with a lease that appeared to have been downloaded from the Internet. My then 10 year old daughter could have done a better job. It was riddled with errors. I felt then that Ronnie was putting his trust in a shady character. I definitely knew that Braun was no lawyer and told Ronnie as much. It didn't seem to matter since he believed that they were getting a new loan from this shyster. I didn't question my brother any longer but could not shake the uneasiness I felt after looking at that lease. It served its purpose, and the children were enrolled into school; but even the school's secretary noticed the error-riddled document. Looking at Braun's business card, my doubts were confirmed that the word "lawyer" belonged nowhere in the same sentence as this man's name. My friend Elaina, who was a realtor, called Braun. He refused to speak with her. This too was a big red flag. In hindsight, there were clear signs from the outset that something was not right.

Ronnie and Melissa moved to El Paso, Texas as planned and we moved into our new home. Almost immediately people started showing up at the house looking to serve them notices. One person said that Ronnie and Melissa had not paid their mortgage in months. I called Ronnie about the visits, and he told me that Braun was handling everything. Someone came nearly every week. Mail came from two banks which I was to forward on to Braun; to whom my brother was still referring to as his lawyer. Despite these notices, we had settled in quite nicely into the house. The children were so happy in their new rooms, with their new schools and happy with their new friends. My husband was in his element in the garden out front, planting shrubs and all kinds of flowers; he learned he had quite the green thumb.

Fast forward to Thanksgiving; we would celebrate our first, and only formal, dinner in our own home. We had a guest come up from Caroline County to stay with us. I had furnished every room in the home except the dining area, but we made it work just fine. Our guest room was very comfortable for our family friend, complete with a large television and cable to boot. The Monday after Thanksgiving, a sheriff's deputy showed up to serve a summons to Ronnie and Melissa. They were not there so they could not be served. I got worried and called Ronnie right away. He said as always, Braun would handle it. I asked him about the mortgage and Ronnie assured me that it was being paid. That was such a relief to me, because we were struggling to pay the rent. Add in the high utilities for heating and cooling we were barely making it. But again, we were in our own home, and we felt the sacrifice to be there was worth it. The deputy returned while I was out and left the summons taped to the door. I called Ronnie right away and he again tried to assure me that all was well. All was not well, as we would find out a week later.

I came home from depositing the rent for December into Ronnie's bank account to find a notice on the door. The notice stated that the property had been foreclosed on and sold at auction; and the occupants were to vacate immediately.

My heart sank to my feet. I was devastated and called Ronnie right away. Ronnie called Braun, who was still running his con game, and tried to blame me for not getting paperwork to him. I was not having it. I informed Ronnie as things were happening. Then I thought, "Wait a minute, what was happening to the money we were struggling to send Ronnie every month?" I questioned my brother about that and he tried to assure me that the mortgage was in fact being paid. I did not buy it, but I wanted to give him the benefit of the doubt. So I checked to see if there had been a misunderstanding with the two different banks that my brother used. How naïve! I assumed that Braun had advised Ronnie and Melissa to stop paying their mortgage as so many people were doing with the burst of the housing bubble. Not only was this bad advice, it is also unethical unless you are filing for bankruptcy. My brother and his wife thought they would get easy money from us, and they did. We never expected to live anywhere for free, because we would have had to pay rent or a mortgage no matter where we were. But we were fine in our cramped, two bedroom condo. We could afford the rent there and were truly looking forward to someday moving into an affordable home. When all of this happened, we had the good credit we needed to qualify for and purchase this home.

Ronnie and Melissa saw suckers, and dangled a hook in front of us. We took the bait, and they took our money. It is as simple as that. When they proposed that we move in with a lease option to purchase the home, they did not disclose that they were not making the mortgage payments. That they knew the house would go into foreclosure; this constitutes fraud in my opinion. Legally they did not break the law, but Ronnie and Melissa did know they were not making their mortgage payments. They involved my innocent and unsuspecting family into their schemes. I am certain they did not claim the money they received from us as income to the IRS. Whether or not they broke any civil or criminal laws, they broke a moral law in my mind. For this, and all their actions, they will have to give an accounting to God.

I contacted the new owner of the home who assured me that the title company had done its homework, and he had in fact, purchased the home at an auction that had been publicly announced. He gave me several phone numbers to call to verify the information which I did. I called Ronnie one last time to ask for our money back. We had to leave our dream home and were now technically homeless. I called my sisters who were just as heartbroken as I was. The person I did not call was my husband. This fiasco happened on a Wednesday and he was due to speak at church later that evening. Had I told my husband, he would not have been able to present his lesson. So I waited until church was over and broke the bad news to him. My poor husband was in a state of shock. I hurt so badly for him. He had a blank look on his face as if he had been stabbed in the heart. He had indeed been stabbed in the heart and in the back by members of my own family. We had to make some pretty quick decisions as the new owner of the home decided to come and meet with us to discuss options.

I asked my sister who lived nearby to come over so she and her husband could be witnesses when the new owner came over. When he learned what had happened, he saw that we were true victims in the worst way; and the culprits were members of my own family. We actually found it odd that the new owner said he saw this all the time, with strangers and families alike. Again, how naïve we were! The new owner saw how nicely I had decorated our home and felt sorry for us. He suggested that we file a lawsuit against my brother and sister-in-law in court. What saved us from having to vacate right away was that fact that we did have a "lease", if that is what you want to call it. After doing some research, we found that many renters were being forced to vacate their homes because they had fallen victim to unscrupulous landlords -- even though they had paid their rent on time every month. Under the *Helping Families Save Their Homes Act of 2009*, the new owner had to honor our lease until June of 2011 with a caveat. He had the option to raise the rent and make it even more difficult for us to pay to live there. Had he chosen to live in the home, we would have had 90 days to vacate. The new owner made it clear that he wanted to sell the property right away. He did not raise the rent; in fact he actually lowered the rent by $500.00 because he was a man of compassion, and knew we had been victimized in this situation. We still had to pay him for those remaining months. We could no longer afford the same house we had more than qualified to buy just six months earlier.

Our credit spiraled downward from there as it had taken two hits from our car payment being late. Payments made late due to paying rent to Ronnie. We had to swing into action. We had no idea what we were going to do. My husband was already dealing with so much stress on his job, that this pushed him over the edge. Normally he could have dealt with anything on his job as he had done for 12 years, but he could not get over the loss of our home and felt like he was not being a good provider. We were both extremely upset at ourselves for not running the other way when presented with this proposal by Ronnie and Melissa. How were we going to move our things? Where were we going to go? I was so embarrassed I just wanted to disappear.

By January 2011, with my husband under so much strain and fearing a heart attack because of his previous heart trouble, I suggested he quit his job. We were going to be starting over anyway, so why not start fresh somewhere else? I had wanted to return to Alaska where I attended the university in the 1990s; so I suggested we relocate there. My husband had never considered relocating there before, but after this fiasco he consented. We felt we had nothing left to lose. There were always positions there for which my husband was more than qualified. He applied for an open position and got it. Now we were faced with how to get to Alaska. We decided to have an estate sale because we needed to move quickly. We made a "whopping" $3,000 on everything that we had worked hard to acquire over the previous 14 years. $1,600 of that went to the woman who organized the sale for her fees. It was sad to see our nice things practically given away, or stolen. Some of our things just could not be accounted for with so many people in and out of the house the day of the sale. Reality set in that we were really leaving that house. If Ronnie and Melissa had just done a simple Internet search on Chandler Braun, who by now had stopped returning Ronnie's calls, they would have found all kinds of accusations and complaints against him. They may have even found that the

Maryland Attorney General was investigating Braun's company. I don't care that Ronnie and Melissa were scammed by this shady character. I care only that my family was pulled into their financial shenanigans and seemed to have paid a much higher price than they did. They have in fact gone on to buy their own luxurious dream home in Texas. My family did not deserve this! "Undeserving" became our new name. My family has been severely hurt.

Did Ronnie and Melissa even stop to think about our children? As much as we tried to hide it, the kids knew something was terribly wrong. Whether or not it was my bouts of crying and coded talk, or packing up our things, they knew something was amiss. Our daughter did not want to leave her new school; she had dedicated teachers there, and she loved it. She did not want to leave the new friends she had made. Even our autistic son said he did not want to go to Alaska on his last day of school. The time finally came for us to head out. We said our goodbyes to neighbors, friends and church family. We packed up what would fit in our car, shipped some ahead to the post office via general delivery, boxed the rest and put it in storage where it remains. We headed out for a trek that would take us across the United States and Canadian countryside.

The roads were not as bad as I had imagined, but they were treacherous enough once we started driving on the Alaska Canada Highway. It was a different hotel every night until we finally made it to North Pole, Alaska. We did not plan properly at all because we were in panic mode, and made a rush decision because we needed to be out of that house.

Going to Alaska did not work out at all. We stayed in the Hotel North Pole for twelve weeks while looking for a home to rent. My husband was able to start his job and the children were enrolled in their schools. That hotel stay cost us a fortune. It did help a little that the staff became like family to us; and we met some other nice families while there. I finally found a place and we settled in but ran out of money. My husband's salary was considerably less than what he made in Virginia, and half of what he did earn, went towards medical benefits. This left us short for rent every month. During my husband's brief stay with this particular employer, two of his subordinates did nothing but mistreat and tried to set him up for failure. He began to resent the job, and never forgot to thank Ronnie and Melissa for putting us in this terrible situation. It is true no one told us to hike up to Alaska, but fact of the matter is, had we not moved into that house in the first place, my family would still be in Alexandria, VA. We would not have been displaced in the middle of winter.

Speaking of winter, the greater Fairbanks area was coming off a season of the harshest weather the city had seen in years. It was still cold when we got there, but within a month, the ice was gone and we had daylight all day and night. The summer weather was good for us, but financially things were getting worse. I had to reach out to my family and friends for assistance. My other siblings stepped up to the plate to help us out but we had to make another change.

My husband had applied for several federal jobs across the country and started getting interviews. By January 2012, he had interviewed with several federal agencies as a clinical licensed social worker and was receiving offers from around the country. When the offer came from Los Angeles, we decided to accept the job and move to California. But the new job did not pay for relocation and so we were in yet another predicament. We had to leave some of the few things we had acquired behind. We packed all we could in the car and headed south to Haines, Alaska. We put our vehicle on a ferry and sailed down to the Canadian border at Washington State. The children were happy to leave Alaska, as my daughter simply could not adjust. There was some bullying at her middle school where she only made a few new friends. My daughter still missed Virginia terribly and all I could do was hold her when she would cry, "I want to go home, I want to go home!" I tried to explain that there was no home to go back to. Her anxiety was only relieved when I told her that we were leaving Alaska. The children did not like having to ride the bus to school in temperatures that got to 51 degrees below zero anyway. In Alaska, the bus came every day so unless they were sick, they went to school.

There are two things we really miss about our sojourn in Alaska; the beautiful landscape and the awesome members of the church to whom we had to say goodbye. They were absolutely wonderful!

When we got to Los Angeles, the people at the new

church welcomed us with open arms. A couple of the sisters reached out before and after we arrived to help make our transition smoother. We had to stay in a hotel for nearly a month while we tried to find housing in a nice area of West Los Angeles. We were in a rush to get settled because the children had been out of school for three weeks. We finally found a place to rent, and got them enrolled into school. The move to Los Angeles was as difficult as the move was to Alaska because we had so little money. I had to once again call on family members who were already stretched thin, for assistance. They came through for us. Even Ronnie and Melissa sent $500 to help us get into the apartment, but only after some intervention from my parents. We are still struggling in our day to day existence, but if Ronnie and Melissa were to return more of the money we gave to them, we would be in a much better position. No chance of that happening though, so I won't hold my breath waiting. I am thankful for the help, but I have to balance that against everything that has happened to us. Ronnie doesn't think that he nor his wife did anything wrong and will not acknowledge their part in displacing my family or for our financial ruin.

It will take years to rebuild our credit. Ronnie believes that we should be happy with what little money he sent back. I say it was about $4,200 total and he says $5,000. Neither amount is adequate seeing that we spent well over $15,000 to get into and maintaining that house. I guess I could be happy if we did not have to sleep on air mattresses, or if I had a decent set of pots and pans. I would be happy if I my children had been able to get new school clothes. I suppose I would be happy if I had enough money to buy gas and groceries at the same time. I would be happy if I did not have to pick and choose which prescriptions I would fill because I didn't have enough money. We are getting to get back on our feet; but it was to be a long, slow process, and recovery would not happen overnight. We have a string of unpaid bills that we plan to pay when we can. Some people understand our situation. Some simply did not care and I understand that, because after all, business is business. But now, we are living on Faith that God will protect, guard, and guide us.

We have learned some valuable lessons and will continue to count on our faith and prayer to get us through. Because of our forgiving nature, we have forgiven my brother and sister-n-law. I have to admit it was hard. I was bitter for a while, given to fits of crying because we lost our car, or didn't have enough money to make it to the next pay day. I still have to look at my children and explain why they cannot go to even some of the cheapest of places at times. I explained to my daughter that first year that she would not be getting new school clothes.

There have been no music, art or karate lessons. We still have to budget everything and live paycheck to paycheck like so many other Americans. But I am determined to help my family recover and move forward.

Today, I would still feed my brother if he were hungry. I would help in whatever capacity I could with no strings. I can do that because I am a Christian and that would be the Christian thing to do. I have learned to look for the positive things in all situations now. Good can come from almost any tragedy. The fact that we are now in Los Angeles, California is actually a blessing because of the opportunities here.

I don't know how else we would have ever had the chance to move here from northern Virginia. My daughter and husband had done some acting in Virginia and they both have expressed continued interest in entertainment. My husband belonged to the Actor's Center in northern Virginia and my daughter had gone on many auditions with Linda Townsend Management in Clinton, Maryland, and booked some jobs. There are no guarantees but Los Angeles is the place to be for exposure to opportunities in show business. Who knows what will come of it?

The best blessing so far is that California is considered an "Entitlement State". For my autistic son, this means, he did not have to languish for years on a waiting list as he did in Virginia for a Medicaid Waiver, which allows supplemental resources to assist those with autism and other disabilities and their families. In 2005, he entered the list at number 2056. He was finally awarded the waiver in November of 2013 long after arriving here. Of course we had to forfeit the waiver because we were no longer there in Virginia. Now someone else on the list can be awarded this benefit. Thanks to California law, there are no waiting lists and my son was immediately eligible for services after an initial intake process. Although this entire transition has been painful for us, we are thankful to God that my son can benefit from these resources.

There will be recovery for our situation and we intend to see it through. We have moved on, yet we are still feeling the ripple effects of this family tragedy. Some members of our family do not want us to share our story and keep this all quiet. My questions to them are, "Why should we **not** talk about what happened to us since we were scammed?" I don't see why Ronnie and Melissa should they be protected. Whether or not the nay-sayers want to admit it, my brother and his wife are directly responsible for my family losing our home. I believe life is too short to remain bitter and not forgive, as we are commanded to do. Yes we have moved on, but we are often reminded of what happened because so much is a result of this tragedy. There is so much to accomplish in life, and we know God's purpose for us. Our faith has helped us through all of this. Our family remains split and we have not heard from Ronnie or Melissa in over a year and that is fine. When they want to reach out, we will accept their olive branch. For our family's part, the healing has begun!

My Family Ran Off My Boyfriend

My name is Selena G. About 20 years ago, I had a
white boyfriend named Matt Z. We loved each other very
much and I could see us married. My parents and brother
did not like him from the start and always gave me a hard
time about him. I should not have been surprised because
in my home there was *always* hatred of white people.

When I came home from college, I happened to run
into Matt who was a classmate in high school. We were
not friends or anything but we did know each other. He
invited me for a quick coffee and I accepted. We started
talking and I found him to be quite pleasant. All the
warnings as a youngster growing up never allowed me to
even consider dating a white guy. Matt was so nice that I
was intrigued and found myself wanting to talk longer,
but I had to go. Matt gave me his phone number and I put
it in my purse. I actually forgot about it for weeks and
when cleaning out my purse I found it.

I gave Matt a call and he sounded really excited to
hear from me. He invited me out to dinner and that was
the beginning of our tabooed relationship. I told Matt that
my family did not care for white people but it was my life

and they would just have to accept him. His family on the other hand was great. After a few dates, he took me home to meet them. His mom greeted me with a kiss and hug. His father complimented me on how pretty he thought I was. I was floored because growing up I never thought I would meet white people so kind outside of those faking it at work or school. It was easy to fall in love with Matt.

I had to eventually take Matt home to meet my folks. They wanted to meet the man responsible for my constant smiles and who was taking all my spare time. I had shared with my sister, but did not tell my father, mother or brother that Matt was white. All I could do was pray that they would be on their best behavior. When Matt showed up for dinner, I greeted him at the door. My family stood there in shock for a minute when he came in. And then my father snapped "Oh Hell No!" I thought I had prepared Matt, but even I was taken aback by his reaction. I pleaded with him to understand that Matt was good to me and that I really loved him. My brother jumped up and got into Matt's face. I had to step in between them. My brother yelled all kinds of obscenities and my father joined in with him. They didn't care that my four and five year-old nieces heard every word before my sister could scurry them out. My mother was upset with me, but she did try to calm my father and brother down and get control.

In tears, I apologized and suggested that Matt just leave. Matt was in mid-sentence attempting to tell my folks how much he really loved me and out of nowhere, my brother just decked him. Matt fell backwards with a bloody nose. After threatening to call the police on my brother, I gave Matt a towel and helped him to his car. All the while, we could hear them talking about *that white boy* in our house. I apologized again to Matt and sent him on his way. He told me it was okay and that he would call me later. Matt did not want to pursue charges against my brother, so I let him drive off. When I got back into the house, everything I could muster from my 22-year-old mouth came out. It was a shouting match to the finish and I went toe to toe with my father. He applauded my brother for being a coward when he punched Matt. I refused to say another word to my brother in protest. In the end, my dad won as he planted a guilt trip on me that I found myself buying. I cried the entire night.

Matt and I went out again, and I thought I could redeem my family. But it was not to be. He actually proposed marriage and wanted to take me away. Matt was not used to that kind of violent reaction from anyone. I told him that I couldn't cut my family out of my life like that. So, we ended our relationship right there. That was a decision I would regret for the rest of my life.

I went home to languish in my misery. My father and brother would bring up that white boy from time to time and remind me that I was never to even think about getting with one. I remained silent for years. Even after graduating and moving out, I allowed that control to guide my relationships. I went out with all kinds of black men. Some were educated, some were not. Some were good and some were bad. Some had good jobs, some didn't work at all. My folks didn't care as long as he was black. By then, my sister confided that she made the mistake of having two babies with black men who were both losers and would have gladly traded places with me and Matt. She listened to my parents and chose bad black men, but she was so young and didn't understand that she could have had a future with a good man and was now stuck as a single mom with neither of her children's fathers involved. My parents don't even care that my sister did not get married; they just didn't want us with anyone but a black man. Who cares if he didn't have goals, or a means to support his children? He just better be black - good guy, bad guy or indifferent. My sister told me I should have fought for Matt and if that meant never speaking to my parents and brother again then so be it.

Over the years, I stopped dating completely and except for my sister, I started seeing my family less and less. I wanted to be alone but not lonely. I was still hurting from my decision to choose my hateful family over someone who was the love of my life. A few years ago, I saw Matt at the mall. I went up to him and said hello. He gave me a big hug and introduced me to his lovely black wife and beautiful children. They looked so happy. For the longest time I thought, "That could have been me!" I was again filled with regret. I should have married him and left my family behind for the benefit of my future happiness. There is just no other way around it. Matt loved me and I could have been married with my own family today.

It took years, but after a few sessions with a relationship coach, I slowly came around. My confidence level is higher now and at 43, I can still look forward to finding love with a man who loves me; and maybe even having a family. I now know it is never too late to find a good man and be happy. I don't know what race my husband will be, but if he is not black, I am totally prepared to leave my family in the dust as they have not changed. I allowed them to rob me once; they will not do it again.

Lorraine Spencer

Take this Bread

My dad recited the same Bible verse, Matthew
26:26 every Sunday during Communion, "While they
were eating, Jesus took bread, gave thanks and broke it,
and gave it to his disciples, saying 'Take and eat, this is
my body.'" Soon after communion, that is when the
offering plates were passed around and the real "bread"
that my dad was mostly concerned with, was the giving.
At the young age of 7, I had no idea that this hard earned
money given by the people of the church was actually
financing my brand new swing set, pool, sand box, and
my brothers' custom basketball court. I had become
accustomed to this lifestyle. Nice presents for my
birthday, big Christmases and shopping sprees. Mom
always acted as if everything was just fine. She never
skipped a beat. My life was as normal, if not better than,
any other 7 year-old; at least that is what I thought.

I was 9 when my mom filed for divorce. Things had
progressed from bad to worse at my house. Mom started
sleeping in my room at night, which really infuriated my
dad. He was such a control freak. Everyone in the small
town of Lewisburg, Tennessee, thought he was the best

man ever. I mean he was the pastor after all and the most self-righteous man they had ever known.

It was a Sunday night when mom and I planned our great escape. Dad came in reeking of alcohol. He burst through the door in my bedroom and stood over my mother in a state of rage. I witnessed the entire thing. You see, I had started sleeping with a knife underneath my pillow out of fear that my dad would someday try to harm my mother. It was only a butter knife but I kid you not, the way I had planned to use it was to poke his eyeballs out if necessary. He then jerked my mother from the bed and demanded that she get out of the house. I jumped up and slid my feet into my house slippers and followed my dad as he pulled my mom out of my room and down the stairs. After he had dragged her out of the house, he finally let her go and we ran up the road. It was a very dark, humid night and my newly pressed hair quickly turned into a large afro. I, with my pajamas on and my mother in her house coat, began the journey of leaving our old lives behind. When we stopped running to catch our breath, I turned around and looked back down the street. I could see my dad in the front yard ripping out all of the pages of my mother's expensive nursing text books. My mom exclaimed, "We are never going back, never!" I was happy. I had grown tired of my dad being so controlling. I was so proud of my mom. She was in the process of finishing her nursing degree as well as trying to gain her independence.

We walked several miles until we made it to Renee's house. Renee was one of my mom's classmates in nursing school and, for the most part, knew everything that was going on in our house. She knew that my mom was ready to leave my dad. Renee welcomed us into her house and made a place for my mom and me to sleep. Mom braided my hair into two cornrows and reminded me that my nappy hair would not be an excuse to skip school and that I would be going to school the next day. Renee was Caucasian and definitely didn't have a hot comb in her kitchen drawer, so the chances of getting my hair straightened was slim to none.

Mom and I were only able to stay at Renee's house for a few days. My dad found out where we were and kept vandalizing Renee's car and mailbox. Mom couldn't allow Renee's family to be in danger so the only choice she had was for us to move into the projects. I was so excited to be moving into the projects! All of my friends from school lived there and there was a lot to do. Also, I finally got to ride the most popular school bus number 73 to school. But mom was not okay with us living in that neighborhood and she worked tirelessly as a nurse tech and completed her degree to become a registered nurse. My mom's accomplishments really pissed off my dad. He even broke into our house one night when we weren't home and slit my mom's waterbed and stuffed clothing and material into it. He stole my bike, winter coat, and took all of the food out of the refrigerator and put it into the washing machine. He did anything and everything just to make it harder for my mom to gain her independence. Mom called the police department and they took the fingerprints on the window. But the detectives investigating claimed that they were unable to match up the fingerprints to my dad's but I didn't believe them. In a small town like Lewisburg, Tennessee, all of the government officials and "who's who" are all a part of a secret society, kind of like a small town illuminati. They all had each other's back.

Nevertheless, none of these obstacles stopped my mother from being an outstanding mother. She obtained her nursing degree and made all of my childhood dreams come true.

I must admit, being a preacher's daughter and seeing what happens behind closed doors has made it difficult for me to believe what most pastors like to portray in the church setting. It seems to be very prevalent in today's society that we hear of scandals involving very well known, respected pastors. My childhood experience has pushed me away from joining the stereotypical African American churches in the South. Although I know that my tithes and offering are for a bigger reason than how my father used it for, I am still tainted by his actions. But I choose to bless others with my earnings in a different manner. Right or wrong it is a decision I have made.

The Black Patent Leather Shoes

That day will never die, although I have spent most of my life trying to forget it. It was a bright and beautiful fall day, and I was playing in the front yard of my maternal grandmother's house. Inside, my aunt Diane was watching television and babysitting my youngest aunt, Marquice. I don't know why I was outside alone; but I'm pretty sure it had something to do with the fact Marquice and I did not get along. It's amazing the details of childhood a person remembers even after forty-six years; and playing outside alone—that particular day—is vividly in my mind.

Marquice and I were born just four months apart. My mom and dad had been married for almost four years, and my maternal grandmother was not married at the time of her pregnancy. Mothers and daughters in dual pregnancies were typical in poor families back in the day—aunts and uncles raised together with nieces and nephews. Such was our norm. What bothered me most about Marquice was she never liked me. She did everything possible to make my life a living hell, and she was encouraged by her mother and my aunt, Diane. Being a child with perpetual forgiveness to dole out selflessly, I did my best to treat Marquice kindly. Don't get me wrong. There were times when she pushed me too far and I retaliated. Whenever I did retaliate, my grandmother chastised me and that began my realization of unequal justice.

This particular day, my aunt Diane sent me to play outside alone. I don't recall what type of clothing I wore that day, but I must have looked like some Southern, cotton-picking, slave baby because when my paternal grandmother drove up to the house, she grimaced. I knew that disapproving look, and it made me very sad. I was about three or four years old and playing in the dry dirt was my favorite activity. I loved wetting the dirt to make mud pies, climbing trees, and playing jacks. Being outdoors was my escape from the torment of Marquice. However, my paternal grandmother interrupted this play day, and she was not happy with my appearance.

My Grandma Sammie Lee called my name, and I rushed over to the driver's side of her car. My uncle John sat in the front passenger seat, and my aunt Cynthia sat in the backseat behind my grandmother. Grandma smiled and told me to get in the car because she was taking me shopping. I was so happy. I felt lonely and going shopping with Grandma was going to be so much fun! Although I looked like someone had rolled me in flour and stuck my finger in an electrical socket, I was going shopping!

With his famous, bright, white smile, Uncle John got out, picked me up, and helped me into the backseat. I climbed in and sat next to Cynthia, who was also only a few years older. Even as I write this story, tears well up in my eyes because of the happiness and joy I felt when my Grandma Sammie Lee picked me up to take me shopping. Who knew that special day would end with one of the most horrible childhood experiences I had, leaving its indelible mark on my psyche.

I don't recall my Grandma Sammie Lee talking to my aunt Diane and telling her where we were going. I was oblivious. All I cared about was going to downtown to Macy's to shop with my Grandma, uncle, and aunt.

When we entered Macy's, everything seemed so big and tall—the people, mannequins, signs, etc. It was almost overwhelming, especially for a small child. Nonetheless, I was overjoyed to be surrounded by so many beautiful things. Taking me by the hand, Grandma Sammie Lee walked me to the ladies room. Once inside, she took her handkerchief, placed it under the running faucet, wet it, and cleaned my face, hands, and legs. She reached in her purse, retrieved a brush, and brushed my hair into a ponytail. When she was satisfied with my look, she led me back out into the department store.

Grandma Sammie Lee led us over to the little girls' dresses. She told me my daddy had sent her money and wanted her to buy me a beautiful dress, matching socks, and black patent-leather shoes. There were so many dresses and they were so beautiful! I tried on yellow-laced, pink-ruffled, white-pleated, and pastel-green, cotton dresses. Grandma, Uncle John, and Cynthia laughed as I pranced and modeled for them. I was grinning from ear-to-ear. I felt so pretty—even prettier because my daddy wanted me to look pretty. I liked the white dress most; but Grandma decided on the pink dress. She told me the ruffles made my bowed-legs look prettier.

We headed over to the shoe department in search of the black, patent-leather shoes. There were so many, but I quickly noticed a pair with a bow on top. They were so beautiful—with a rounded toe and shiny, silver buckles. To finish my new wardrobe, Grandma picked out laced, pink socks. She took me back into the restroom, and changed me into my new clothes and shoes. She added a pink ribbon to my ponytail and we left Macy's. For the first time in my childhood, I felt pretty. I was the happiest little girl in the world.

Before returning me to my maternal grandmother's house, Grandma Sammie Lee treated me to a burger and fries. Of course, I could not have catsup or mustard; but the food was still delicious. As we drove back to the house, I leaned my face out the backseat window taking in the sunshine, cool breezes, and blue skies. I had not expected such a wonderful day. I was so happy. I felt loved.

Grandma Sammie Lee pulled up to the familiar curb. Uncle John got out, leaned his seat forward, and reached for my little hand. He picked me up, grabbed the shopping bags containing my old, soiled clothing, and carried me to the door. My aunt Diane answered, and didn't seem happy to see me. That was okay because I felt pretty. I stood inside the screen door and my uncle walked back to Grandma's car. He waved as he got in. Grandma and Cynthia waved, too. I smiled, waving back. Then, they were gone.

My aunt Diane told me to come to her. She looked at me, but she wasn't smiling. She never said a word. She opened my shopping bags and dumped the dirty clothing and ratty shoes onto the living room floor. Taking me by the arm, she pulled me to her, turned me around, unbuttoned my new dress, and pulled it over my head. Then, she told me to sit down on the floor. Taking each foot, she removed my new black, patent-leather shoes with the shiny, silver buckles. Stripped down to my clean, ruffled underwear, Aunt Diane told me to put on the dirty clothes she had dumped onto the floor. Maybe she didn't want me to get my pretty dress dirty. I was a dirt magnet after all.

What happened next left me confused and devastated. Aunt Diane called Marquice over and dressed her in my new dress, socks, and black, patent-leather shoes. I couldn't believe what was happening. What had I done? I was a good girl. I didn't cause trouble. I was not mean to Marquice. I admired my Aunt Diane. She was beautiful and funny. Why did she want to give away my pretty things? I began to cry. Aunt Diane told me to go outside and play.

As I sat in the dirt-filled yard, I stared out toward the curb where my Grandma Sammie Lee had picked me up and dropped me off. She wanted to make me feel pretty and I indeed felt pretty. But now, I sat in the original soiled clothing, alone again with dirty tears streaming down my face. Soon, Marquice stood in front of me, taunting me wearing my pretty, pink-ruffled, dress and black, patent-leather shoes. I wanted to throw dirt on her, but I didn't want to get my dress dirty. My aunt threatened to beat me if I told anyone, so I never told my mother until sometime in early 2012.

I will never get over that experience. Cruelty at the hands of relatives seems worse than at the hands of strangers. I was only three or four years old; and this incident has left my heart broken for more than forty-six years. I did not know the meaning of hate. I still loved my aunt. She died of breast cancer in 1989. I was active duty Navy and could not make it to her funeral. Her oldest daughter told me my aunt kept asking for me. All these years, I wondered if she asked for me because she was sorry for stealing my joy that beautiful, fall day. I wonder if she ever realized that by removing my black, patent-leather shoes to put them on the feet of Marquice, something inside me had changed forever. I will never know, but whenever I see a pair of black, patent-leather shoes, I have to steal away because the tears flow freely.

I Just Want My Babies

My name is Terrina Williams. When I was 15, I became pregnant. My mom was so angry when she found out at 4 weeks. The father was a guy at school who was clueless about life. His parents wanted me to get an abortion and be done with it. My mother agreed with them and dragged me off to the clinic to have it done. I begged her not to make me do it, but to no avail. I went into that cold place with those cold people. Nobody cared that I was crying. I was told to get undressed and given a gown. Mom turned on me and didn't care that I was scared. She just told me to take my lumps and pay for trying to ruin her life. Ruin her life? I would not understand that comment until much later. I endured a painful procedure and was told to get up and get dressed as if nothing had happened. They had just killed my baby.

I couldn't sleep and I had nightmares. I could not talk to mom about anything, which is why I went right back into the father's arms. In a few months, I was pregnant again. I told my mom who proceeded to slap me near senseless. I got a speech about how much she gave up to raise me alone and I was not doing this to her again. I was dumbfounded and told my mom that she could not make me get another abortion. She told me that I was getting one and that was all there was to it. She made the appointment and I went quietly. When we went inside the clinic this time, I cooperated until I saw the same cold doctor who killed my first baby. I screamed and made such a scene that he ordered me out of the room and the clinic. I was happy and relieved but my mom had a plan for me. Later that evening, my mom told me that I was going to stay with some people who could help me. I didn't know who, it didn't make sense; but I thought she had relented and accepted that I was going to have a baby. I wanted my baby, so I was happy to go anywhere. I spent the next few months at home, but one day I had a plane ticket to Salt Lake City, Utah, waiting for me. I had to leave school, pack some clothes, and get on that plane.

I arrived in Utah unsure of where I was going, but met a nice couple waiting at the airport. They introduced themselves as Ken and Patty. I stayed with them and they treated me nicely and didn't judge me. I often thought about the father of my child and how he was going to react when he saw the baby for the first time. I was sure his parents would love their grandchild. I knew my mom would too, even though she had been so mean. I was enjoying the thought of having a baby to love and who would love me.

A few days before my delivery, my mom came to support me. She wanted to be with me in the hospital delivery room. I forgot about how mean she was and thought how cool that she wanted to see her grandchild born. I knew I was having a little girl and picked out the name "Emily Donna". I was excited to go into labor. It hurt so much, but I was having my little girl. When I saw mom talking to the doctor and nurses, I thought maybe she was telling them to make me comfortable because my epidural was wearing off. Then little Emily Donna started coming, I had to push. Three good pushes and she was there. Mom took Emily from the nurse as soon as she was cleaned up. I thought mom was bringing Emily over to me; but in disbelief, she headed over to the door and handed my newborn off to a woman waiting there. I screamed "My baby, my baby"! Mom told me that there was no way that she was going to raise another baby and that I wasn't either. I was beyond hurt, tired and sore. I just wanted my baby. I wanted Emily Donna so badly. My joy became the nightmares I had after my abortion. Mom asked if the doctor could give me some medicine as if she really cared. She just didn't want to hear me cry. The nurse put something in the IV in my hand and I woke up later.

When I woke up, I started crying right away. Mom was there and told me again that she had signed papers for a closed adoption. I had never known such cruelty before or since then. I had no say or control in the matter. I felt I could raise my child and be a good mother. Mom wouldn't even let me hold my own baby. She told me it was best because she did not want me getting attached. Attached? That was just too much too bear. It was done and there was nothing I could do. I was only 16.

Two days later we left for home. I barely spoke one word to my mom. I return to school embarrassed. I did not think that my mom had one compassionate bone in her body. Did she think she was saving me? No. Mom made sure I had what I needed for school, but no more. Mom warned me that I had better not get pregnant again or I would find myself kicked out of our home. I don't know what she was thinking to tell me that. I was intimidated enough, but I couldn't go through another pregnancy or deal with what would come with it. I never saw any more boys while in school. My baby's father avoided me after telling me his parents thought the adoption was the best thing for everyone. They did not care; they didn't want their precious son tied down and throwing away his future as they accused me of trying to do. I only saw him a few more times before he transferred high schools. I have no idea where he is today and I don't care.

I finished high school, and left home at my first opportunity. I paid my own way through college and joined the Air Force. I gradually cut off all contact with the woman who gave me life. I felt what she did was unforgivable. I would speak to my aunts and uncles and some cousins, but had nothing to say to my mom. I wondered about my own dad and why I had never met him. One day, I asked for help from an aunt I trusted. She gave me all the info she could about my dad. She told me that mom did not tell me the whole story. I only know that he left and never paid a penny toward supporting my mom and me; so I was told. My aunt told me that mom got mad at my dad and walked out on him, taking me with her, and she vowed that he would not see me growing up and she made good on her promise. How do you get away with that? Mom had stolen me from my dad and now not one, but two babies from me. I could never do that to my husband and three children.

I am close to retirement after 24 years in the military, and when I am done with my service, I hope to find my father. My children and husband don't think I should wait a moment longer to start looking for him; or their sibling who I was forced to give up for adoption. Maybe they are right. I still miss my first baby too. I love my children more than anything but still feel so empty from the loss of my first two babies. I'll never get over my mother being so cruel and heartless. She stole a part of my life and never showed an ounce of regret. I was only a teenager, so young. But I knew I would have made a good mother as I have been for my other children. Emily Donna would be 30 years old today. I hope she had a wonderful life. My heart will ways have a void even though I have forgiven myself. I just want my babies.

My Niece Attacked My Child

I used to have my always, last minute prepared, gem of a baby sitter watch my children. Our regular sitter was sick, so my sister Denise helped me out again because I had to go to work. Denise called me at work to tell me that my son would not quiet down and wanted some suggestions on how to calm him down. That was a first. Denise dealt with screaming kids all day at her in home daycare. I asked to speak with my son C.J. He was only 3 years-old and not too happy about leaving me or my husband Jim's side anyway. Denise put my son on the phone and he did quiet down enough for me tell him I would take him for ice cream if he was a good boy. It did not work. C.J. started crying again as soon as my sister took back the phone. Feeling a little anxious about my baby, I decided to leave work early.

As I got to my sister's house, C.J. ran up to meet me with his arms held out, and I extended my arms out to pick him up. I got all my children in the car and strapped C.J. in his car seat. My son was so happy to see me that nothing else really mattered. I needed to get C.J. and the girls home. Denise came out to meet me and reported that C.J. did eventually calm down and spent the rest of the afternoon in her arms. I thought that was strange and later found out why.

On the drive home, I pondered what I would make for dinner. As soon as I got in the door, I handed the baby off to Jim who made it home before I did. He went to change C.J.'s diaper. I put on my flats and went to the kitchen. I had barely started retrieving food from the refrigerator when I heard my husband shouting my name, "Trudy!" I ran to the baby's room and was horrified at the sight. The tears just streamed as I saw my son's thighs red, black and blue. He had obviously been spanked. But this was not a regular spanking. C.J. had been beaten. My husband demanded an explanation that I couldn't give. But I was on the phone to Denise right away. I asked her what the hell happened to my son. She told me that her 8 year-old daughter Zina was playing and tried to discipline C.J. and used a wooden spoon on my son before she could stop her. Furious doesn't come close to what I was feeling. I was hurt; and I hurt for my baby.

I questioned my daughters Gayle and Leslie who were 5 and 7 to see if they saw anything. Leslie said that she saw Zina hit C.J. and told her to stop. Then she said that Zina tried to hit her too but Denise came into the room and stopped her. Gayle said that Zina bullies them all the time and hits them when the grown-ups are not watching. I hung up because my sister tried to make excuses for Zina. I went back to my dinner and could hardly concentrate and just put all the food away. My husband and I discussed what to do.

My husband wanted to call the police and make a report, which we did. I didn't care about hurting Denise's business. If she is going to let this happen to my baby then what about the children who aren't even a blood relation? Denise must have sensed we were going to take action and called us back to plead Zina's case. We were unmoved because she attacked our baby. My brother in law did not abuse my sister or Zina. Where that behavior came from is a mystery. I did tell Denise that we would not be going back to her for anything. Our minds were made up because that bruising was so horrible.

We took our son to the emergency room. C.J. checked fine by the ER doctor but he verified that C.J. must have been hit pretty hard because of the bruising. The doctor made C.J. laugh while he checked him and gave us some liquid pain medicine for him.

The police came to the hospital and we gave the report. No charges were filed or anything, but it did get my sister investigated. She eventually shut down her daycare because she could not protect children from her little monster named Zina.

That little monster grew up to be a big monster. Zina dropped out of school because she was always being suspended anyway for fighting and just overall bad behavior. The writing was on the wall. Zina could not even cooperate in an alternative school. She was such a bright young lady and could have had anything in life that she desired with a little hard work. Her parents continue to bail her out of jams, clean up her messes and make excuses for Zina's behavior. I stopped counting how many times she has been arrested. Zina was destined for prison. Zina has caused her parents heartbreak time and time again. They are caring for Zina's own 2 year-old.

Zina has not been allowed in my home for years. I do not feel bad about the Zina ban, because my children's safety and well-being had to come first. I could not and would not give her another opportunity to victimize my children.

I have no qualms about my position when it comes to protecting my family. I do love my sister and I have long forgiven Denise for making excuses for Zina when she attacked my son seven or eight years ago. I have actually tried to be more understanding as a mother because sometimes our children will do things that we as parents have to address and sometimes fix. But some things we cannot fix. As a Christian family, we pray for Denise and her family often. I believe that you can be forgiving, yet keep a safe distance from those who would cause trouble or harm you and your loved ones. In fact, you have an obligation to protect and put your family's safety and well-being first and that is just what we did.

Sibling Rivalry after All These Years

My name is Dennis Stuart. Since elementary school, my brother Dan and I have been very competitive. It was more on his part to best me at everything we did. We made good grades, played sports and worked hard on every project we were assigned. Both mom and dad were teachers, so it was a given that we were competitive. I got a bachelor's degree in engineering and Dan as well, but Dan one upped me and my parents. He got a Bachelor's and M.D. degrees. By the time we were in our mid-20s, I was so tired of this silly rivalry game, but Dan was as competitive as ever. I was concerned that our younger twin brother and sister were starting to become like Dan. I just observed and mentioned to my parents that Dan took love competing with me for some reason. My mother did sometimes have my father step in when she thought Dan was going a bit too far. But it had been years since I had heard her say anything to my father or Dan about his need to be out in front on everything. I hope they would stop this with the twins.

I stopped protesting and let Dan go on with his games. I stopped telling him anything about my plans because all he would do was find a way to diminish them and throw insults about what or how he could do something better. I remember when I said I was going to take guitar lessons. Dan said that he had already taken guitar lessons years ago and learned piano too. Why couldn't he just say something nice? This was the scenario with everything I did or said.

When I started dating my wife Courtney, Dan was nice to her and thought she was pretty, but he was determined to get a prettier girlfriend. The girl he was dating named Anne, was very attractive and super nice despite Dan's obsessive behavior. He opted to trade her in and go for a prettier girl. Dan found Jin in the gym where he worked out every day. She is actually half Chinese and half British. Jin is smart, getting a Master's degree in International Business and will one day run a Fortune 500 company. Jin stood up to Dan. They debated a lot but seemed to genuinely love each other. I didn't get involved in their lives at all. I was too busy courting my wife and preparing to propose after about ten months. I made the mistake of sharing my plans with mom. After all, it was mainly mom who taught me how to treat my Courtney and win her heart. Overjoyed, mom told Dan how happy she was for me. She even smirked that she would be getting some grandchildren sooner than she thought. Dan could not stand the fact that I was so happy and getting married before he would, so he set out to sabotage my plans.

About four weeks passed. On the day that I proposed to Courtney, she accepted over a nice quiet dinner. We invited our families to dinner the next night to officially make the announcement. Everyone came including Courtney's parents and two younger siblings. Dan and Jin invited her parents who were visiting from Hong Kong. I announced that Courtney and I were officially engaged and planned to be married in about a year. My father stood up and toasted us. He blessed our engagement with all kinds of compliments and told us he already loved Courtney like a daughter. Courtney's mom cried and her parents came over to hug us both. Mom cried too and told her future in-laws how happy she was to increase our family by five people. I tried to ignore Dan's fake smiles but wondered how he would try to out-do me. I expected him to say something nice even if he was insincere. Well it only took ten minutes and Dan made an announcement of his own. He stood up, congratulated me, and announced that he and Jin were also engaged and getting married in Hong Kong, in three months.

Everyone was in shock but applauded Dan and Jin. He did it again. Dan's competitiveness now included innocent parties. My parents and I knew exactly what he was doing and I was seething, but I contained my anger and was determined not to let Dan completely ruin our night. Dan totally manipulated the situation by asking me to be his best man. Not only did he try to steal my joy, Dan was bullying. I quickly turned the attention back to our announcement and said that Courtney would be planning her dream wedding and that I was leaving everything up to her. Courtney stood up and announced that I made her the happiest woman in the world. She also showed class in congratulating Jin. I finished my dinner in a fake, festive mood.

Needless to say, I had a talk with my parents the next day. They calmly advised me to indulge Dan. I did not intend to indulge Dan. I was planning my life with Courtney and was taking her to a new housing development so she could pick out her home on a plot of her choosing. My goal was her happiness and her happiness alone. I make a good income and was looking to finance a new home. Plans to go to Hong Kong did not enter anywhere into the equation. My mother was horrified and said that I would be playing Dan's game if I did not go to his wedding. What? I was flummoxed. I had to stand my ground and insist that financially I didn't see where I could do it. Financial sacrifices would be for my future family only. I would not assist in Dan's bullying of me or manipulation of my parents. My dad volunteered to pay for Courtney and me to attend the wedding. I did not want to do that either but they insisted. That meant that my parents were now paying for themselves, my two younger siblings, and for Courtney and me. I was uneasy and did not like it one bit.

Courtney was beside herself with a beautiful glow planning our wedding. She showed off her ring to everyone she met. I was happy to make Courtney as happy as she made me. But we had to switch into happiness mode for Dan and Jin as it was time to go to Hong Kong. We all went and enjoyed ourselves. It was Courtney's first trip abroad and our first trip to Hong Kong. It is a beautiful country. The wedding was quite lavish in a hotel ballroom. It was splendidly decorated with bright colors and crystal chandeliers. They even had life-size wedding photos of Dan and Jin covering an entire side of the reception hall. Jin's father is an executive who could obviously afford all that luxury. While I stood with and supported Dan, I could not help but look at Jin and wonder if she knew that she was an unwitting party in my brother's quest to outshine me. She was happy so I just left it alone.

The wedding was very lovely and Courtney was really happy for Dan and Jin. The festivities were going well until Dan told Courtney that her wedding would not be as extravagant but would still probably be nice. I did not take the bait but Courtney politely told Dan that she was planning her dream wedding but that the exterior was ultimately insignificant. She further stated that even if we decided to go to the courthouse to get married that she would still be just as happy because she loved me and as long as we were together, she was happy. Dan had no follow up to that and never brought it up again.

We got back home and on with our plans. Dan and Jin built at a new development close to where Courtney and I were building. But of course they had one and a half acres and built an enormous seven-bedroom, five-bath, three-car garage home. I was not trying to out shine Dan.

Courtney and I planned for our budget, as she wanted to be a stay home mother when the time came. We had to live within our means. Our four-bedroom, three-bath, and two-car garage home was more than enough for us. Before we knew it, the house was done and our wedding date was a mere three weeks away. Courtney moved in our home and started decorating. Mom, her mom and her friends had a blast helping her out. Jin also came over to help. Courtney was in her element at the bridal shower thrown for her there.

Our wedding venue was marvelous. Courtney's wedding planner booked us a mansion in the meadows of southern Maryland. My sister, who somehow had grown up overnight, was a beautiful bride's maid. Courtney was radiant in her beautiful gown. I was overjoyed to lift up her veil and see those beautiful brown eyes filled with so much love. Nothing would ruin my lady's day, so I thought. I had even given a pass to my mother's pleading to have Dan as my best man. I feared he would pull some stunt, but looking at my bride put all those thoughts away.

After the wedding, we took photos, changed clothes and went into the reception. My mom greeted us with hugs and tears and that even made me a little teary eyed.

Two hours later my mom was still crying. I went to give her a hug and told her it was okay to be happy but she should stop crying and start dancing. Mom then told me that while Courtney and I were taking our wedding photos, Dan and Jin told her that they were expecting a baby.

My joy turned into outrage as I realized that Dan actually did it again. WHEN WOULD THIS RIVALRY END? This time he tried to ruin my wedding. I found out that they had told Courtney but she was a real trooper and carried on as if nothing happened. She was a delight to watch, a true blushing bride in all her glory. If Courtney could let it go, then so could I. We continued celebrating for several hours and mom continued crying off and on. I knew she could hardly wait for a grandchild and was getting her wish so I didn't want to ruin her joy either.

When Courtney and I returned from our Honeymoon, our lives went on as usual. We are living our American dream. I include my parents and the twins who turned out fine by the way, in our lives at every opportunity. But I keep my family away from Dan and his family.

I refuse to allow Dan to hurt my family as he has tried to hurt me over the years. I avoid confrontations and simply won't subject my children to being compared to his. My parents love all their grandchildren and that is good enough for me. I have moved on. My wife and children are great and I am happy with my life.

Reflection

The question that weighed heavily on my mind was could I truly be forgiving if my brother and sister-in-law never asked for it, or even offered a half-way decent apology? My family remains split, but I have moved on. I had to remember my purpose and that life really is too short not to enjoy it and appreciate our blessings. Is it hard? It can be; almost every aspect of my family's life is still impacted and will be for some time to come.

Recovery will be a long and hard road, but Faith has to account for something. Prayer is indeed powerful. I will always have prayer as an ally. Through good days and bad, I can pray at any time. I pray for my family—all of them. All I can do is live in the spirit of forgiveness and do my part. I am reminded of Ephesians 4:32 - Be kind and compassionate to one another, forgiving each other, just as in Christ God forgave you. (NIV)

Where there is conflict, there can be resolution. But not all conflict is resolved. Sometimes we just have to accept the fact that healing may have to come via alternative means if it comes at all. Forgiveness and resolution does not mean further victimization and we indeed may have to love from a distance.

When family does you wrong, some may forgive and move on while others may not as life is not so simple. I wish all the contributors comfort, healing and resolution – whenever and wherever possible.

ABOUT THE AUTHOR

Lorraine Spencer finally realized her dreams of becoming an author earlier in 2013. She loves writing short stories, and is a guest blogger for Black Women Deserve Better, Beyond Black and White, My Beautiful Life Magazine and the BWE Bloggersphere.

She has several blogs including Autism Anthem, Wonderhys, and Through Elijah's Eyes.

Lorraine has published several books: Princess Sapphire, Gem of the Land; The Spider in My Mommy's Car, I Like Polka Dots on My Pizza; The Mama Toe and Do Squirrels Eat Pizza?

Lorraine Spencer is a relationship coach and is the founder of Swirling and Marriage™. Lorraine loves children's books and is in her element writing poems and adventures for children. But she enjoys for multiple genres as well. Lorraine holds an M.S. in Human Resources Management and Development from National Louis University (1997) a B.S. in Western Language and Literature from Excelsior College (1993) an A.A degree from the University of Alaska (1991).

When not coaching, writing or doing research, Lorraine spends time with her husband and children who all serve as her inspiration.

www.ingramcontent.com/pod-product-compliance
Lightning Source LLC
Chambersburg PA
CBHW060353050426
42449CB00011B/2959

9 780615 872698